WE KNOW THIS PLACE

ISBN: 978-1-60801-225-1

Cover photograph of Sunni Patterson by Niala Howard.

Cover photographs of street tiles by Infrogmation of New Orleans:
"Hewes" available from: https://flic.kr/p/2kh8NU2.
"Apricot (Now Walmsley" available from: https://flic.kr/p/2kh8NB3.
"Sidewalk Street name tiles" available from: https://flic.kr/p/UCfpkR.
"Cherokee at Maple tiles" available from: https://flic.kr/p/Rv5bAH.

Cover and book design by Alex Dimeff.

Portions of this book have appeared previously in the following
publications:

"My City Ain't For Sale," (as "Not Fa' Sale"), commissioned for the
Homecoming Project by Junebug Productions, 2018, and reprinted in
I Am New Orleans, edited by Kalamu ya Salaam, the University of New
Orleans Press, 2020.

"We Know This Place," originally printed in *Standing Up to the Madness:
Ordinary Heroes in Extraordinary Times*, edited by Amy Goodman and
David Goodman, Hyperion, 2008. Reprinted in *American Quarterly* 61.3,
2009, and in *In the Wake of Hurricane Katrina: New Paradigms and Social
Visions*, edited by Clyde Woods, the Johns Hopkins University Press,
2010.

First edition
Printed in the United States of America on acid-free paper.

RUNAGATE PRESS

UNIVERSITY OF NEW ORLEANS PRESS
2000 Lakeshore Drive
New Orleans, Louisiana 70148
unopress.org

WE KNOW THIS PLACE

poems

SUNNI PATTERSON

Dedication

My Mama...

Faith-filled
Sharp-tongued
Big-hearted
Truth Teller
Shit Talker
Prayer Maker
Patcher Up-er
Healing Herb
Cup of Tea
Shot of Gin
Communion Wine
Eucharist
Holy Spirit
Holy Church
Holy Mother...
    Keep me covered
Your prayers...
    Have hugged me tighter than your arms sometimes
Your ways...
    Give mine more meaning
Your days...
    Forever honored
You...
    Forever cherished

My Daddy… (here but not)

Tears gather as I write.
My way maker.
My Masquerade in Heaven.
I haven't erased your voicemail messages.
I listen to one every holiday.
But nothing compares to the messages you leave me now.
Ever present.
Every lesson is etched in my heart.
Your face stitched in my skin.
There is not one day that passes where you do not cross
     my mind.

In honor of Ancestors past, present, and future…
Find favor in me… And whatever/whomever my heart/
     mind/hands touch.

In service and gratitude forever,
Sunni
(Soul, IyaNifa Adenikee, Imolerun Ewosanfe, Mama)

CONTENT

PREFACE

This wasn't easy. Wasn't just a "gather the poems and submit" kind of thing. Maybe it could have been. Maybe. But it was not. It was months of everything from death and disease to the divine in-betweens. Everything except this. Baba Kalamu and everyone on the UNO team so patiently and compassionately expressed an understanding worthy of an award. Although, some of it was probably mixed with a little "bless her heart." You know when people say that, it's not always a compliment.

Truth is, these reckoning times rocked all of us to the core. As a Spirit worker, Priestess, Coach, Community Health Worker, and Artist, these COVID years have been full and busy and empty and demanding and hopeful. However, as I realized when I spoke with Chelsey, my editrix at UNO Press, I move rather slowly when it comes to doing things for myself. It's easier to serve others, to give. But this work required more of me for myself. More than I could give after a day of divination and sessions with young couples eager to marry. This isn't poetry for a foundation training lawyers in Critical Race Theory. It's not work for a rapper who needs your words to ensure a video is played on BET, or a community event bridging the gap between science and art.

I mean, it was hard, as much as Baba Kalamu would say, "Look, dis ya first book. Make it easy. Just use summa da poems you already got; ones we familiar wit'. Don't make it hard." Or my favorite: "Sunni, befo' you get home, you gotta get to first."

That one spoke to me. I come from a baseball family. My grandfather, Albert "Buddy Red" Lombard, started out as a bat boy for a pretty well known team in New Orleans, the Algiers Giants. He then grew to be a pitcher; struckout Jackie Robinson once, too. He also played semi-pro ball in Canada. My Daddy was a catcher for a few teams in New Orleans. Just about every bar room had a team. My Daddy's most memorable team was called Dee's Ghetto Pirates. Dee's was the name of the bar—in case you were wondering.

All that to say, here's me finally getting to first. Rather, here's me putting myself first. Thank you for the reminder, Baba. I'm already looking forward to the next book.

Dear Poet

If it weren't for you,
this world would be lackluster and mute.
These hearts would only be heads
too heavy laden with too many thoughts & none of them
  bearing the mark of love.
Who else gon' do what you do?
Who else gon' be a safe haven when the destructive ones try
to paint our heaven the color of their hell?
Who else gon' speak a word to shift the world as we know it,
  into a world of our dreams?
Who else gon' speak to our dreams?
Nobody but you, Poet.
Nobody but you.

1. MEDITATION

Come By Here

Come by here, Ancestors,
  With your fire & fierceness
  Your protection & peace
  Your music & laughter
Come by here
  With your life affirming principles
  Your destiny shaping words
Come by here
  Where we aim to expand our existence & further our mission
  All in the name of what is right & real & good
Come by here, Ancestors,
Where you are welcome

Ancestor Invocation

Ancestor
Breath
Bridge
Carry us over tumultuous time
You who can hear and answer with quick remedy
 Ready before we ask
You who can speak through tongues of trees
& fire
& water
Earth cannot hold you
We pound the ground
& You appear

O, Ancient Ones
You who can make lightning strike
with the flick of a skirt
You who can make tornado turn with the spin
& span of hips
Take us there
To the place of knowing
The hall that leads to the doorway of You
O, Holy Ones
You of the first light
You who know the potential of possibility pulsing in the dark
Deliver us unto our gifts
You who have sunlight in your fingertips, touch our drums
Make us hear the rising
Make us move
A steady stomp
A choir of voices so majestic
Heaven hides us in a tapestry of light

We are stars, blankets of wonder
Sky bright eyes
Seeing the invisible, visible
You who have returned,
You have turned our faces to see ourselves
& we have found You again
In places we would have never imagined
You make our limits infinitely long,
Our vision clearer with eyes closed
& even there
You still stand in full color
Vibrant & eager to serve

Crossroads

there is a place
where head meets heart
meets world
meets every point in between
the line where sky meets water
meets earth
meets flame

oh, wayfaring wanderer,
sojourner of truths,
caution on the road—
for One is always watching
with cowried colored eyes
wide with child like wonder
innocent and ancient
secular secrets
sacred medicine
manifested matter
connects us one to another

while we are here

in the middle of the way
at the entrance of the gate
pleading
   do not confuse me
in this world of possibilities
of choice
of chance
of intuition
of logic

of knowing
of prayer

where 3 become 1
where past meets present
meets future
where seed
meets soil
meets plant
where One is always watching
guiding us to enlightenment
mediating our existence
while we resolve within ourselves
our heavens
our hells
our hiddens
our seens
and every point in between
all while being here...

in the middle of the way

Oshun

in honor of my spiritual godmother, Chief IyaNifa Osunmonife

My Mother's house is a river
I am lured to Her door
and immediately I am humbled
It is here She administers Her cool water cure
abundantly pure
I see my face in Hers
clearly
my Mother is a mirror
and when I am real still and quiet
she shows me Her secrets
my Mother, the diviner

O, royal and divine One,
shine Your golden rays across our faces
trace our insides with Your light
allow me flight on Your wings
carry me to the feet of the Father
to a place much farther than the sun
take me to the land my Ancestors come from
show me how You spoke peace to five women chained and
   bound in Zanzibar
with iron so heavy and tight around their necks
their heads almost collapsed—
but at the mere remembrance of Your essence
they survived

Tell me how you spilled from the eyes of Anastasia in Brazil
when her mouth was filled with metal for urging
others to break free of their fetters
You, Mother,
Better to me sometimes than I am to myself
fan me with Your feathers
make sweet the path
make me forget I ever had a problem
my Mama will take any obstacle
wrap it up in the finest gold
throw it over Her shoulder
real brave and bold
in just a matter of minutes
watch a healing unfold
   I swear
my Mama is a miracle

With just the touch of Her tips
barren women are given children
the sick become healed
I am filled with delight at just the mention of Your name
Maferefun Oshun!
it is You
so often misunderstood
so often I wish I could stand atop the roof of your house
and shout of your majesty
O, Golden Lady
it is Your face
in feather
and fan
and brass
and water
You are distinctly divine

And I can't say enough times
that when you come to my Mother
you better come smart
because Her honey is sweet
but Her blade is sharp
oh perfect protector of children
great defender of women
gracious lover of men
She comes to serve you Her love on a platter
    eat up
there is plenty more where that came from
She is the generous one
will prepare a table before me in the presence of mine enemies
surely goodness and mercy shall follow
my Mama is a leader
a champion
a queen
come let Her hide you
come and get your feed
you can stay until you're full
when you are here
there's plenty room

In my Mama's house
I am humbled and honored to be
in such a holy space
I place You high, Mama
glad that I am one of Your daughters
You anoint my head with Your waters
my cup runneth over
and before you know it
I am back at Your door
to offer a salute
and give You thanks once more

Yemoja

Great gush of morning,
Amazing spring of truth
She who enshrines Her children with love
Be our fence
Pull us to Your bosom
where safety sounds like a heartbeat
We hear You in everything
Feel Your flowing waters pulsing through our veins

Mama, we are home where You are
Great Star of the Sea,
Lady of the Land
Queen of Heaven,
Triple crowned Goddess
7 layers veil Your glory
7 seals set Your secrets
Who can speak of Your mystery?
None but those who have basked in Your blue,
Twisted ribbons around full bellies
trusting their babies will make it to this side
Safe and healthy and whole
Who else but those bearing melon and molasses pleading
at Your shore for stability and protection?

You who are unafraid to pull machete on our behalf,
then bathe in the blood of Your enemies,
Who can defeat You
when Your children have been threatened or harmed?
O, fierce and matchless warrior
Pearled perfection, coraled grace
She who chides Her children when they have gone astray

The One who answers when She pleases
Big Mama of the house
She whose children are fish
The one whose riches are too numerous to count
Your wonder goes on
You show us that everything is possible
that there is no limit to love
that our abundance is as vast as Your waters

Who can tell where the ocean ends?
none but You
The Fashioner of Forever
Mystic Mermaid,
Mist of Magnificence
Your scent is in the wind
Captured and carried right back to You
Make us over
Wash us new
Hail the Universal Mother
All praise unto You

Oya (Wild Women)

Wild Women walk with buffalo
have lightning on their tongues
flywhisks as weapons
Wild Women walk with machetes
with wisdom,
with grace
with ease
Wild Women have hurricanes in their bellies
releasing a flood of lessons
Wild Women fly free
watch their ways,
how they rip and shred
who can understand Her
this winding Niger river of a woman
One who is unafraid to tear away
only to roam
and then become the wind
She who speaks in gusts and cyclones
blasting us back to high ground
high consciousness
She turns
   and so does the world
feel Her spinning
spanning several lifetimes
hear Her speaking
sparking alarm
see Her dancing
summoning the dead
resurrecting new life
Heaven hears Her
knocking on the door

safely transporting the ones who call for Her assistance
Wild Women open portals to new worlds
new speech
new dreams
oh, dearly beloveds
so dearly departed
from the ways of the Guardian
beware
for Wild Women are not to be tamed
only admired

just let Her in
and witness Her
set your days ablaze

2. OBSERVATION

My City Ain't for Sale

... not my potions
or my spells

not my crawfish
or my crabs

not my brass
or my ass

   ain't none of it fa sale

not my cemetery
or my temple

not my land
or my love

not my "plareens"
or my "huckabucks"

   ain't none of it fa sale

you peeping toms and sallies
you wisconsins and nebraskas
you thieves and tax collectors

   ain't nuthin ova here fa sale

not my theater
or my park

not my music
or my art

not my soul
or my heart

ain't none of it fa sale

you bandits and you con men
you dumpster divers and hoodlums
keep your eyes off my prize

cuz ain't nuthin over here for sale

not my shotgun
or my cottage

not my bar rooms

none of my houses
if you ain't hear it in the last announcement:

AIN'T NUTTIN OVER HERE FA SALE

not my Parrain
or my Na'nan

not my "Aintee"
or my Granny

my Paw-Paw
not none 'ah my family

   I'm tellin ya
   ain't nuttin ah' mine fa sale

not my sinners
or my saints

not my coulds
not even my can'ts

don't see the picture?
lemme grab my paint
make it pretty, pretty
use proper language:

   There is nothing over here for sale!

not my culture
or my crown

this city has had enough of you clowns
wanna build it up
but keep me down

   oh, anything to make that sale?!

you want me to give you all I got
you want my window and my pot
Lawd knows it ain't a lot...

but it's mine...

  and it ain't fa sale

you don't know me or my kind
my heritage, my history, my line...
my dignity, my legacy, my pride...
some things just ain't up for buying

so while you gentrify and plot
while you calculate and allot
of all the things, put this one on top...

AIN'T NUTTIN OVA HERE FA SALE!

When Black Girl Magic Evolves into Black Woman JuJu

when power exudes from pores

when heart expands

when listening is done with more than ears

bone deep

and boundless

a blood tied sacrifice

a walking Altar

offer more than your words here

after all

I birthed your mouth from my own

we communicate in placenta

in parable

in places before this one

my sisters sit in circles sifting stories of old and future times

re-telling the records of ancient beings

foretold us of a time when we would have to re-mind you
  of your return back to the beginning

re-member you whole when limbs are humpty dumped on
  battle fields

and the only thing that can put you back together again

is a mother's moan

or a woman's word

when your blood free flows in the street

or your feet trample hearts too heavy to hold

or too delicate to touch

we, gatherers of tears

seamstresses of men

turn sorrows into gin

pour libation and petition Spirit on your behalf

oh, if you could remember

if only you knew

the jungles I have gone through

the fires I have eaten

the waters I have spilled

all in hopes that you would float right back to me

that you would feel the warmth of my fluid

that would hear the hum of my poem

that you would give a reminiscent smile

that you would wake up walking

wielding a sword

chopping every illusion and obstacle in the way of you
  getting

back to yourself

and not because of me

but because after all

you remember all of you

remember the parts you left that left you incomplete

remember the pieces of the dream

remembered your skin and scent and longed for yourself

became your own water

your own thoughts

your own you

then saw me with eyes speaking a language normally
reserved for flowers and I heard you

touched me in a way that made me remember my plant life

we have spanned life times

life forms

forged a way out of rock and sky

sea and mineral

seed and leaf

you and me

A mirrored magnificence

where each stage of life

is a page of sacred scripture

our presence alone is a healing balm

& tincture

is salve

is cure

we are becoming something more

something bigger than before

morphing into the beings the primordial ones spoke of

we're out of space here

we're outer space here

we're traveling grace

we are larger than thought

we fill the atmosphere

we are cyclical

we are linear

we are particles parting and dividing

then finding ourselves at every turn

there you are again

there i am again

meeting you for the first time

and here we stand

arm in arm

hand in hand

circles expanding and contracting

exploding and compressing

extending and constricting

forever weaving in and out

we were always told

about how you'd return

how it would be daytime

how the sun would be at its peak

how you would smile

how it would light up the sky

and how we would dance the dance of celebration

because the warriors have returned in full glory

Savior Shit, Save Your Shit

But...
did it ever occur to you that I didn't need you to save me?
... didn't need you to rush in, smearing your ego-tinged
politics across my face?
Did it ever occur to you that I like my Black like I like my
Black?
... and that I enjoy myself in all my Blackness?
Does it offend you when I don't show appreciation for your
efforts to make me hate my Black,
only to make me take on your judgmental jargon and jive?
Does it hurt you when I don't want to mingle with your
new demons because I am still
traumatized by your old ones?
Did it ever—I mean, *eeeevahhh*—occur to you that I maybe
don't want to be around you
   because YOU
   remind me a whole lot
   of THEM?

They Wanted Her

They wanted her
piecemealed
paper-mache'd
practically broken
limp-like
and loveless

a litany of exaggeration,
they wanted her
low
and high
flat
and wide
filled with all of their empty
they wanted her to be more like them,
not knowing
that her conception was immaculate
that she was birthed in sandalwood scented river water
with sweet sapphire honey touched tongue

she was too much of a mouthful for the greedy
just a small amount of her was more than they could stand
they wanted her bland
and barren
unspirited
unafrican
uncultured
under siege
in the streets
they wanted her face down
ass up

hands cuffed
and ankles strapped
they wanted her
knowing she would never want them back

they wanted her holy
baptized in her divine
they wanted her secrets
her pearls to swine
they wanted to unravel the mystery of her design
fascinated by glory
hypnotized by her kind
they wanted her complete
they wanted her whole
though they came fractioned
half hearted
half souled
with no regards
and no knowledge as to who she really was

oh, if they knew her
praise songs would rain from the clouds of their eyes
clearing the vision
bathing the heart
they would bow every time they saw her
be their best selves when she was around
if they knew her
knew she was the glue to their revolution
the life flow of blood through their veins

if they knew her
she would know

Artist in Exile

1.
This is not a eulogy
not an obituary for the dead
not a story of those who once were
but of those who live
those whose spirits walk
and work
and fly
those who toiled and taught
and loved
those who fashioned seeds into okra and greens
flipped wood into house
into sweet shop
into church and marriage steeple
into refuge for the addict and downtrodden
into haven and heaven

Their voices permeate the present
piece together space and time
a quilt made of "Maroon" blood and railroad spikes
huckabucks and wine candies
Kool Filter Kings and Hail Marys
…of prayers hummed and moaned
…of flood water and flickering flame
…of execution and exile
…of return

2.
Water always finds a way back to itself
to its source
I, too, have stumbled my way back to you
at some points on all fours
Knowing you would receive me

*"blessed be the wayfaring warrior, the forlorn traveler who still loves
me even though I have let you down. My new lovers were so enticing,
forgive me, my child, for I have sinned against you"*

How can I not forgive you?
When I know your parts have been fondled by hands
   heavy with hell in their tips.
I forgive you.
You taught me how to do that

3.
Since your tearing apart,
I have lived through
about 49 seasons
one marriage
the birth of 2 living children and another due around the
   summer equinox
I wonder and work often at mending your heart
and your memory
I, too, need help sometimes
Do you forgive me for the way I have allowed others to
   enter your gates
most with their shoes still on
more with pale privilege still on their tongues
And tits
And penises
penetrating the inner core of your being?

Believe me:
we tried
with hoop skirts, bloody heads, spells masked as psalms and saints,
Saturated grounds in holy oil and prayers
Attempted to sync your heartbeat with the rhythm of our drum,
with the hammer of our heels on the pavement
with the snake of our arms
we tried

and we drowned.

4.

Every birth needs water
needs dark
needs to be honored and remembered
every one for its different coming forth
Each birth bears its own map and blueprint
Its own name and vibration
Its own self...

5.

When we emerged after the Big Rains
many were surprised
thought they'd never see us again
thought the dead would always be dead
Not knowing our Easter is everyday
Not knowing that wherever we rose in pick-a-city, America
Our Red Beaned Mondays would still exist
Our Fish Fried Fridays would still come at the end of each week
Our music would still play
and heal
and hold

How easily they forget what we are made of
forgot how we would move between swamp and concrete
forgot how we made home in the wettest of places
foreign and far-fetched
barefoot and unstitched
forgot we put ourselves together from a million fragments
   before
the apple never falls far from the tree
"Grand" never far from the "Petit"
the lessons still course through our veins
still flash in the dark parts of our existence
some things never change… or leave
and some of us never forget

6.
I remember the way like the back of my hand
know pathways and trees by heart
tuned my ear to the tone of your aura so even when the
   familiar
things do leave,
I can still find you
And you will still know me

Oh, some things… they never change
and you, you are one of them

Black Boy

With all his majesty and might
his brilliance and his beauty
his black and his blue,
 "Boy"
still slips from their lips when they address him
still lingers in the velvet of his dreams
the seen unseen
Black boy fighting for manhood
in a world that still sees through Jim Crow lens
them love him in his place
separate
away
torn
disconnected
passive
submissive
and shuffling
now turn that shuffling into dancing
'cause you know them love Black boy dancing
and singing
and balling
love Black boy strength
but don't love Black boy
don't love Black boy
don't love Black boy
now him drifting in the wind
searching for himself
in places that never allow him to be himself
so now Black boy scared of his own shining Black reflection
but we don't call you a son (sun) for nothin,'
Black boy radiate sacred wonder

we see you shining star
in the mirror of your own eyes
and ours
your manhood is manna
is sinew
is potent
pure
Black boy proud of the Black man he has become
we see you
a pillar in the place of crumbling remains
Black man you reign/rain
an effervescent dew that wakes the world
we honor you
and bear witness to your power

3. DEDICATION

Akoma

Akoma Day was created by Montsho and Nwasha Edu

And it was written:

"Be transformed by your love.
Be moved by holy intention.
Be steadied by your faith;
And take heart as you trod.

This was the instruction given to the two who became one.

Be an altar for one another,
A divine point of attraction and forgiveness
Of offering and reception
Of ritual and routine
A reciprocal exchange
Flowing in and out
over and under
True Akoma love is a covering from the brutal winds of lack
A protective shield in the time of internal struggle and attack
It is both the ability to endure and endurance itself

Knowing what you practice often,
you tend to perfect
Make a habit of love
Of positive creative expression
Of on-purpose, mountain-moving faith
Of unbridled belief in the Essence of all that is Good
Gaze in the mirror of your partner's eyes
See yourself as your Self
as your partner
as one

As reflection of God
Where connection supersedes critique
Where gratitude and appreciation are constant companions
Oh, take heart as you trod!
This path can be filled with
Shards of self sabotage
How many times have you cut your hands
picking up parts of your heart from the floor?
Careful as you collect your pieces
A conscious coming together is not always painless,
But it is possible
To move as a unified force in the world
An expansion into Oneness
Transforming our lives and all who look on
From Holy Trinity to Infinity

An Akoma marriage leaves a legacy of Love
A spiritual genetic flowing through the blood
We are not only making humans,
this is how you make gods
On earth as it is in Heaven
Where our collective destinies dance
Where our culture lives and thrives
Where Akoma Day is everyday
And Black Love courageously shines."

This was the word for the two who became one
For the brave souls who understood
that even a feather becomes
heavy in the presence of an unfettered heart.

Ancient Love
For my Husband

Where do I begin?
shall I count the ways?
shall I count the amount of sunrises and sunsets?
count the days?
the nights?
the time?
let me honor you without a limit

if this were just physical
time would play a much bigger part
but, dear heart,
we are much more ancient than that
sanskrit sacred
full moon flavored
the power of creation fills this space
fuse ourselves one
each move, a tune
each tune, a tool
this is the true art of alchemy
the holiest matrimony
most mystical marriage
a mantra of magic
ascended masters like craftsmen
your life like my ladder

push me higher
make me taller
no catching if I fall
knowing I'm falling on love
or in light

pure joy
unbridled bliss
this is walking on wind
a pilgrimage past our former selves
into the future of a new return
Ancestors rejoice
Angels applaud
cosmically calling us home

and here we are
present
perfect
on purpose
a continuous stream of prayer
all in praise of the sacred
where lovemaking is equivalent to meditation
this is not for the uninitiated
only those willing to go through the transformation
for a time
we are formless
feather-like light
there is no end to us
we are much more ancient than that

For Mama Jen (*Community Book Center*)

Some people visit libraries
Others become them
Become home for those seeking everything a word can give
Reflection and action
Beginnings and endings
all wrapped up in a few syllables and sounds
We have found Community with you
when other places have eaten us up, spat us out, and
   expected us to keep
the slime on our faces
You clean us up with paragraph and prose
Line after line
Time after time
You give us back ourselves
Show us what it means to be in love with the souls of Black
   folk
Because you know us from cover to spine
And every page in between
We are open books in your presence
Ready for the reading
And the wisdom
And the wit
And the cuss out
And the love up
And the shut down
Lawd, Mildred's child has become everybody's mama
Did you imagine your life to be this way?
Did your Liberty Street dreams come true?
Did you see yourself as who you are?
As compass and conductor
Walking us through uncultivated mental terrain

Carrying us over troubled waters of emotion
You point us to the Norths of ourselves
Activating an imagination out of this world
You are scientist and surgeon
Through critical analysis, you cut through bullshit with
    expert precision
Then give a prescription to aid in the healing:
    "Ok. For now… That'll be one dose of The Radiance of the
    King *and two doses of* Two Thousand Seasons. *And let me go
    ahead and add a dose of* Caste. *Take as ordered and we'll monitor
    your progress from there."*
Certainly, this is beyond the bounds of books
Beyond the body of letter and shape
This is a call to the literacy of life
A reading of yourself and your environment
A comprehension of the universe and its language
A sharpening of mind
A stamina of Spirit
The ability to hear the unspoken words of another and
    question,
"Where you FROM from?"
In other words,
What is your origin story?
How do you hold it?
And how do you give it away?
You…
You hold out an invitation for all of us to remember the
    beginning
Of how some people, they just visit libraries
And Others… well…
They become them

XX Marks the Spot
(for V and the 1Billion Rising)

though tattered and tired
you...
still glorious and worthy of our praise
double x marks the spot
you healer
you shaman
you sorceress
you dreamer
you mama
you medicine maker
you mambo
and priestess
they tried to keep you silent in the midst of their hypocrisy
tried to lull you to sleep with their cadence of mediocrity
tried to bury your body beneath their misogyny
they wanted you dead
wanted your shrines driven underground
wanted your altars a vanishing vestige
wanted you long forgotten

how silly their attempts

because for every one they try to take
another billion rise
stronger
more resilient
more beautiful
more re-membered
and absolutely unafraid

19

& when they read of this moment
They will see how we endured
& they will wonder how we made it
How we could live through such a time & still smile & create
& celebrate
Even though walls of panic & loss continue
To build up around us

They will shake their heads in astonishment
They will question how we survived without hugs &
    secondlines & community gatherings
They will drum up every conspiracy theory & most of
    them will be correct
They will feel the anger of the era
The frustration of the season
They will pick apart the science & discover to their surprise
There was so much more hidden
This virus was a disguise
They will tremble at the revelation
Tears will come to their eyes
For they will see the essence of being in the living & those
    who died
Oh, when they read...
They will see
How this time provided a shift in foundation & frequency
How it challenged outdated systems & let go of antiquated
    beliefs
How we were forced to grow our courage & practice care
    in the midst of grief
When they research about these days...

From the uprisings to the downfalls
They will unravel the knots & connect the dots
& they, too, will heed the call
With dignity & integrity
Ancestral wisdom & pride
Where creativity & imagination move head & heart to
  alignment
They will know…
Because they will feel
The power & presence of devotion & will
  Of culture
  Of spirit
  Of justice
  Of light
  Of oneness
  Of harmony
  Of divinity & insight
Oh, when they read of this moment…
They will see how we endured
& they will still question how we made it
& we will say...
  How could we not?

4. CLOSING

Interview with Kalamu ya Salaam

Kalamu ya Salaam: When did writing become attractive to you?

Sunni Patterson: From a lil bitty girl, I used to draw a lot. There were always things I couldn't say then. It was also at the time my mother and father would have their arguments and other things going on too. So there were things I felt like I couldn't say the way I would've liked. But I would draw them. That always comes to mind first when I think of how I started writing, even though that's drawing. I would imagine different scenarios and situations and everything. That kind of thinking, that kind of dreaming and imagining, allowed me to flourish and fly. And then I was also writing cards. That was the big thing. I would write get well cards, Mother's Day cards, Father's Day cards, birthday cards from a little girl. So I would draw the picture and do the poetry inside the card. That started when I was maybe five or so.

And then as I grew, I got my hands on something my Daddy had. A lil chapbook by Arturo Pfister. I forget the full name of it now, but in it he had a section called "The Beatitudes." He say, "Blessed be the my-onnaise," instead of the may-onnaise, "and blessed be the chessa draw," instead of the chest of drawers. Now, I thought that was something! I was like, "Did everybody know that this was not a chessa, c-h-e-s-s-a draw?" I was a lil girl running through the house like, "Did you know this? Did everybody know this? You know, why we say it like this?" That was probably my introduction to seeing written New Orleans dialect. It also showed me that how we speak, think, and "be" is different, but worthy of praise.

Even being in church—because that's another place where I was urged to write and speak—it still didn't hit me like it did when I read this thing of "The Beatitudes." Because even within that piece, Arturo wrote about Malcolm and this thing of culture and specifically New Orleans culture. What we knew as life. And then he tied that into this international figure. For whatever reason, that did something for me. It was historical, it was cultural, it was spiritual. It was all of these things that I knew my life to be, because it was like everything that I had moved through myself. From church to theater and plays. Just everything that would sum up what our life was. It was this mixture of literature, of art and culture. And it was like, "Oh this might be all right. It might be good."

KyS: So, this brings a question that you might not have a direct answer for. When did you learn to read and when did you learn to write? Because you could draw without being able to read or write.

SP: Right. That I don't know.

KyS: What school did you go to?

SP: That's a good question. So, my first school was Miss Gwen. That was around the corner from where I am now. I live right now in Algiers. That's where my Momma is from, Algiers. My Momma's side is huge. The Lombard family is a big one. So, my first nursery was there in Algiers with Miss Gwen. She is around the corner as a matter of fact, on Diana Street. And then, from there, I went to my next nursery, which was in the Ninth Ward, where my Daddy is from. It was called Desi-Flo.

KyS: Called what?

SP: Desi-Flo. D-e-s-i-f-l-o. In the middle of the Desire and the Florida projects. So they called it Desiflo. Desi- from Desire and Flo- from Florida. Was inside what was called the "White Building." Was only called that because it was painted white.

I think of Desi-Flo often. I remember my teachers very well. Even the smell of the nursery comes up as I'm talking about it now. I remember playing a lot. The play kitchen was to the left when you walked inside of the space. Oh, now I'm remembering preschool graduation. I had to read something. I just don't remember what it was about. My mama might remember. I'll have to ask her.

So, I went from that preschool to kindergarten, at St. Mary of the Angels, which was also the church I went to. And that teacher was Miss Jones. Miss Jones was a hard teacher. Now, that is when I finally remember writing. And I remember that because if you didn't get something right in this Catholic school, you had to kneel in the corner on rice. We had to put our hands on the table sometimes and she would come over smacking hands with a broomstick. *(Laughing)*

KyS: So, people may not be clear on what you saying when you say "kneel on rice." It translates all over, but they used to put [uncooked] rice on the floor and make you kneel down on the rice. And that sucker would hurt.

SP: Oh yeah. Oh, yes, it would hurt. It would hurt a good bit. It was motivation for sure. But it was still love, I still felt loved, in case somebody reading this is like, "Oh my God. She was abused." No, it wasn't that at all. I stayed at St.

Mary of the Angels for first and second grades. But then, I went to Jean Gordon, because they had gifted classes. They didn't have that at Catholic schools, so I went to Jean Gordon and then Beauregard for junior high, then Xavier Prep for some of my freshman year of high school, got expelled for fighting, and then later graduated Warren Easton high school.

But I know my love for writing and reading was fostered first in the home. My mother was a teacher. My grandmother was a teacher. My aunts were teachers. So, I got it in the home and then in church. Growing up, I was a junior spokesperson for a group called All Congregations Together, I was president of youth groups and all those kind of things. So it fostered a real love for writing and speaking.

Even the priest at church would come and say, "Sunni..."—and I didn't really know what this word meant then—but he would say, "Sunni, I need you to write one of those militant poems. The archbishop is coming and we need him to know about the history of this church." And I was like, "All right. But a militant poem? What is that? What does that mean?" And he said, "You know, the things you already do." I said, "Oh. All right."

KyS: So, there's another step in this process. And this step, a lot of people overlook it as being critical, but I think, definitely, it was critical for me. And that is reading.

SP: Yeah.

KyS: And what you read.

SP: Yeah.

KyS: Can you remember what was inspiring you as a young reader?

SP: So, I loved, loved, loved to read. But my father was one who would want me to read all these other books in elementary school, *Chains and Images of Psychological Slavery*, Na'im Akbar. He tried to make me, but I was like, "Daddy, I just want to read *A Wrinkle in Time*. That's it, I'm not trying to—you know, I like fantasy and sci fi kind of stuff. It wasn't until years later, like years and years later, that I finally picked up Na'im Akbar and all the books my father wanted me to read. I'm also grateful for my elementary school teachers at Jean Gordon. Teachers like Mrs. Gruenig and Mrs. Zimmerman. There I was introduced to Zora Neale Hurston, *Their Eyes Were Watching God*. I used to love getting those Scholastic book papers to order books. *(Laughing)* I wasn't always allowed to get any, but I would love looking through the form.

I was a big magazine person, too, at that time. I think a lot of the magazine stuff probably came because I would spend a lot of time in doctor's offices. I had scoliosis really bad as a child. I had to wear a hard brace from sixth grade on through junior high. I hated it! Twenty-three hours a day at one point. I would sneak and take it off at school. Leave it in my locker sometimes. Eventually, I had to have surgery. So, now I have two metal rods holding my spine together. Anyway, I would spend a lot of time in those places and I would want something that I could roll up quick, like those *Highlights* magazines. I wanted something that wasn't too bulky to carry around then. I remember *The Babysitter's Club* books, Nancy Drew and Hardy Boys kind of stuff. I read all of that.

But it still allowed me, again, to just let my imagination fly, let my imagination go, and that was the biggest part, I think.

Now, let me say this: I still had to read all of those daily Bible scriptures and the Quran. Whatever they assigned in Sunday school or Vacation Bible Study. You know in New Orleans, even though I grew up Catholic, my grandmother and everybody was Baptist. We had a whole lot of spiritual doctrines and teachings to adhere to. *(Laughing)*

It wasn't until I grew up that I realized, "Oh, all these things are different for real."

KyS: So, let me be clear about your reading habits. You read widely. Your father wanted you to go deep into one direction, but you just wanted to read whatever you could find that held your attention at the time.

SP: Absolutely. But I was really just being defiant when it came to my Daddy. *(Laughing)*

KyS: Yeah. You can make me hold a book, but you can't make me read the book.

SP: Right! But then, eventually, I did. And my father, being who he was, would say, "I put that on your desk five, ten years ago, and now you want to read it? Can you imagine how sharp you would have been had you read this when I gave it to you?"

I was like, "But, Daddy, I was seven, all right? I didn't want to read it then." *(Laughing)*

KyS: Let's skip some years now. All these years were critical in your development. You no longer just see the world, now you want to understand the world.

SP: Yeah. Yeah. I don't think that really happened until, maybe, right when I was coming out of high school. In high school I would travel around a good bit to speak in different places for the All Congregations Together group, and being a youth leader, in the choir, and things like that. But it wasn't until college that I said, "Oh, yeah. I can *SEE* some things now." Studying more, reading even more, researching more. I went to Tuskegee. So having these books, and this history, and walking in, say, Booker T. Washington's home, and coming in contact with handwritten notes and letters and things like that from his own hand—that's when things really shifted.

Everything else was good, but when I was able to do that kind of research… Walking through the hospital, places I wasn't really supposed to be in. That hospital at Tuskegee. Seeing there were still the folders, medical records. Stirrups with blood still on them. Syringes. These kinds of things. I was catapulted into a whole 'nother world and said, "Oh. Okay, let's see how much deeper we can go."

You know? So that was a big shift. Going to college shifted my thoughts from New Orleans, into this whole other world, this whole other space. You know, reading about Tuskegee experiments was one thing. Being there on the grounds and actually seeing documents, that was a whole 'nother thing.

KyS: Tell me about reading *The Autobiography of Malcolm X.*

SP: Oh man, that was one of the ultimate come-ups. Like… Damn! So, I have to bring that back to the poem, Arturo Pfister's piece. And also my father. Because Malcolm X was someone he looked up to, and I think a lot of that was due to his life and upbringing. Drugs, hustling, and running the streets, he did that for much of his life… and mine. So now, that brings us to this thing of transformation, right?

So, when I think of this transformation, specifically Malcolm's transformation, I wonder, would he have been allowed to move from Detroit Red to Malcolm X to El Malik El Shabazz to Omowale in today's culture? We don't know what that process would have looked like.

As I'm thinking about this and remembering when I read the autobiography, it didn't make me just think about him, about Malcolm. It made me think about the men in my family, the first being my father. It was a certain empathy, sympathy, compassion, and love that I had for my father, but that also made me have even more love for my mother, and just women in general. To be able to love a man through these kinds of transformations and transitions. What does that do for our hearts and what does that do for our spirits?

When I read the autobiography the first time, it sparked something. Then reading it a second time, it sparked something else. And then giving it to SAC [Students at the Center, a New Orleans high school writing program where Patterson taught] to read, it sparked yet another thought. Malcolm's story was one of such transition and change, it seemed that each time it would come up in my own life, I, too, seemed to be in this shifting time at the same time... each time! So, reading it as a little girl was one thing, reading it as somebody in college was something else, then reading it as an adult who's now charged with teaching the book, and reading it with students who have a similar background as [Malcolm], but they are just discovering him, or just discovering these other sides of him—that was a big thing. Because now you move from this, "Oh yeah, yeah, I've read about him," to "Oh, I feel like I know him." And that's how the students would feel. They were coming into it comparing him to themselves or people in their own lives. There was a growing compassion. A kind of divine understanding that comes when it's read.

KyS: One of my theories is that *The Autobiography of Malcolm X* is a book that African American young people can read—I should say young adults—to understand two things which are not normally put together: the power of transformation and the power of love. And there are a lot of books you can read for knowledge, in the scientific sense, or in a philosophical sense, but that don't necessarily carry the love. There are a bunch of books you can read that have the love, but don't give you the knowledge to deal with this society. *The Autobiography of Malcolm X* is the introduction to how you can, as we used to say, walk on two legs.

SP: Walk on two legs, absolutely Baba, absolutely.

KyS: And I don't know if there is any other book that does that. That teaches someone to love being who you are and to love your people and, at the same time, encourages you to transform and move to a higher state, wherever you started at. It doesn't matter. Move to a higher state.

SP: That is true. Yeah. That's very powerful.

KyS: You know, I think that that's why *The Autobiography of Malcolm X* is so important, more important than any other book for black youth to read.

So, now let's skip a while. I have a question that seems to be unrelated. What was your birth name?

SP: My birth name is Sunni. Sunni Kimisha Mary Patterson.

KyS: Spell Kimisha.

SP: K-i-m-i-s-h-a.

KyS: All right. And it was Sunni, S-u-n-n-i?

SP: S-u-n-n-i. I was born on Sunday, on a pretty, sunny day. My father was, well, we would always laugh and say he was a "nickel and dime Muslim" at the time. People would say, "Why you say nickel and dime?" Well, we say nickel and dime because he was still in the streets. *(Laughing)*

So the spelling is from the Sunni Muslims and also Sunni Ali. And they say he wanted another son at the time. So, that's where Sunni came from. And then they always told me, "You know, you was just so big and yellow and then you had blue eyes, so you know, it just went together." *(Laughing)*

KyS: So, Sunni Patterson, when you graduated from Tuskegee, what did you want to be? What did you want to do?

SP: What did I want to do? I wanted to travel and write and teach. That's what I wanted to do. So, I went to Africa after I graduated. I was supposed to go to Cornell for grad school. My professors tried to convince me to go. "Oh, you can get your Masters and your PhD. Won't be as long as you think." And then I was like, "Yeah, I just don't feel like being in the cold, though. I'm not doing it." They kept saying, "But it's a great opportunity. It's going to be great," and I just said, "Yeah… but no. I'm good." So, I went to Africa with Doctor Jeff.

KyS: Morris Jeff, Jr.

SP: Yes. Morris Jeff, Jr. We did Ghana, Togo, Ganvie, and Benin. After that, the question still came, "Well. What are you going to do now?" My first husband and I got married while we were there in Africa. We came back home, and after a while, was married here in Congo Square. Then after a while we divorced. Typical journey of the American African. Married in Africa, divorced in America. *(Laughing)*

Anyway, I don't know why, but I just didn't feel like going back for grad school. Well, I guess I know why. I needed more Spirit in my experience. I didn't think grad school at the time could give me that. I wanted to get right into teaching. Especially with the community work that we were already doing. And then one day I'll never forget, Dr. Jeff asked me, yet again, "What are you gonna do?"

I said, "What do you think about me going back to school? I want to just go ahead and start teaching now!"

And he said, "Just teach and do grad school later." Now that was the worst thing to tell me. I was already leaning to the "not wanting to go" side. So, "do it later" ended up meaning "do it plenty, plenty years later." I still haven't gone, but I get the urge every now and again.

However, the major thing was to teach. To teach, to write, to perform. Honestly, I just wanted to do anything with a microphone. That was it, from the time I was a little girl. From playing school to having song and dance routines, to reading Shakespeare aloud to my Daddy and uncles. *(Laughing)* That was something he always liked when I was younger. But I had to do it with an accent. *(Laughing)* They would be high as kites. *(Laughing)* Either way, I wanted my work to include using a microphone.

KyS: Spell Ganvie. Spell Ganvie.

SP: G-a-n-v-i-e.

KyS: And where was that?

SP: That's West Africa. It's actually in Benin.

KyS: Okay.

SP: And so in that particular place, they literally live on the water. They live in houses on stilts in the water. Story is, the people of Ganvie were being attacked, and the only time they couldn't be attacked was if they were on the water. So they decided to move on the water. Which is why they live on the water to this day.

KyS: All right. Now we going to make a jump and then we going to jump sideways. The jump is that when I met you... I consciously remember meeting you. You turned up working with SAC at Douglass High School.

SP: Yep, yep. That was not long after college. I was a young teacher. Right out of College.

KyS: And what was that experience?

SP: That was great. It was challenging, yes Lawd, but it was great. It was what I wanted to do. It answered the call for activist work. It answered the call for community building. It answered the call to teach, to perform, and that was a beautiful experience. I started after we came back from Africa and my cousin Tuere was already working with SAC. Douglass was a little like the movie *Lean On Me*. Tough, but still so much love. I'm still close with some of the students. They're grown now.

KyS: So now we get to the social substance of your writing. We have the transforming power of Malcolm X, then we have your whole history of being a performer and a writer. Like you say, you love the mic. And you made all those little cards. And, you are an activist. You put that together, and you get Sunni Patterson, the writer.

SP: That's it!

KyS: Because you weren't just writing Hardy Boys and stuff like that.

SP: No, no. No, no.

KyS: Even though that's what you came up with.

SP: Right.

KyS: But you also came up out of the Ninth Ward, and you also came up with seeing what this society was like.

SP: Yeah.

KyS: And so, even though you liked fantasy, sci fi, and romance, and all this stuff, at some point society as you knew it was what you wanted to write about. But you also wanted to write about transforming our society, because you had the example that transformation was possible—and, more than possible, was necessary. Whether you put it that way philosophically or not, that's the story you told.

SP: Yeah. Yeah. That was it. It's like, yeah, I had a choice, but I didn't really have a choice. *(Laughing)* I think about my parents, my family, my ancestors, now my children and husband. I think about all of the folk, especially those mentors and godparents who would prompt me to write or pray or just think beyond this physical plane.

Even when I think back about church and being told, "I need you to write a militant poem," I'm reminded of how church was the place where I learned about the 1811 Slave Revolt and things like that. We learned about those things in church, not necessarily in school. So the things we learned in church fostered a certain kind of spirituality. A certain belief and way of believing. It wasn't like some, "Oh yes, God is in the sky and he's going to come down." It wasn't that kind of thing. It really was the practical idea of, "Okay. We need this militant poem for Sunday." By allowing that type of speech and thought, I learned that poems were not only offerings, but they, too, were the words of God. So, that kind of service, spirit, and activism shaped me, but it was also already in me, as well. Like in my family. I think about my uncle Rudy, Rudy Lombard, and all of his work with CORE and the sit-ins and the Civil Rights Movement. And then the rest of my family. I think of my mama's prayers and instruction. Didn't matter what was going on, she would always advise, "Light a candle and say a prayer." The only thing that would change is the color of the candle. (*Laughing*) Oh, but she was and still is, a great mix of holy and hood. (*Laughing*).

Like you said, in a sense maybe I didn't know what to call it then. I just knew when something was wrong, I had the obligation to step up. That's just how I was taught. Even in times when I couldn't lend my voice, I would have to write about it or draw it or something. I just knew this was what I had to do in order to be true to myself. To be in my purpose and to be in and of service.

KyS: This interview is a way of people entering into the work of Sunni Patterson.

SP: Okay. You got it. All right, Baba. I appreciate you, thank you.

KyS: I appreciate you. Peace be unto you.

We Know This Place

We know this place...
for we have have glanced more times than we'd like to share
into eyes that stare with nothing there behind them but an
   unfulfilled wish
and an unconscious yearning for life
though death rests comfortably beside us...
at night their moans are louder...
they come to visit the guards at the gate
and they stay until morning
torturing their guilt-ridden insides
the silent cries of the keepers are louder than the booms
   that come from the guns
they use to occupy the space...

And we know this place...

for we have seen more times than we'd like to
imagine
bloated cadavers
floating through waters of a city gone savage
foraging the land for what can be salvaged
   but what can be saved when all is lost?

it happened in august...
29 days in
we are now 5 days out of the only place we knew to call
   house and home
few things are certain...
1. we have no food
2. there are more bodies lying at the roadside than
   hotplates being distributed

or first aid being administered
or recognition as a citizen
14th amendment: X
refugee: check...

And we know this place...

ever changing, yet forever the same
money, power, and greed the game
they suck and devour the souls of the slain
what a feast for the beast at their table of shame
with napkins round necks to catch the blood that drains
   from the flesh they chew
it's hell to gain...

And we know this place...

all too well
dank with smell of death and doom
it hovers
it smothers
no growth
no room
no pretty
no please
just gray
just gloom
just borned me a hope and it died too soon
just juking
just jiving
just living
we just fools...

And we know this place...

decked in all its array and splendor
golden streets with good intentions
capture our attention
gadgets and inventions
pesticide the food supply
flu like symptoms
diabetic condition
a cancer in the system
health on hold
it's a pistol to the temple
go run to the churches
tell Rev it's simple
good works and good deeds is what equals redemption
but tell me please—
Jesus never mentioned—
how do church men get extensions on freedom
while children are being fondled from the Altar
to the streets
then back to the Sanctuary
its kinda scary, ain't it?
to know that both the prophet and the priest practice
    deceit
then come to the people and claim "peace, peace"
they come to the people and claim "love, love"
but where is the peace?
where is the love?
where is that balm in Gilead that can heal the wounded
    soul
or make the half man whole?

I swear, we know this place!

'cause we have vowed before never again to return
but here we are...
back in the desert
dry mouth and thirsting for waters from Heaven

but come, come children
rally round
and maybe together we can make a sound
that'll shake the trees and
rattle the ground
make strong our knees
we's a freedom bound!

And we know this place...
   reclaim the crown
hold to the prize
   never put it down
be firm in the stance
   no break
   no bow
gotta forward on, Mama
   make your move now!
forward on, Baba
   make your move now!
forward, dear children, because freedom is
NOW!